HALLOWEEN

Based on the teleplay by Carl Ellsworth

LEVEL 1

Adapted by: Jane Rollason

Commissioning Editor: Jacquie Bloese

Editor: Fiona Beddall

Designer: Dawn Wilson

Picture research: Emma Bree

Photo credits:
Cover photo and inside photos provided courtesy of Fox.
Page 36: J. Sohm/Corbis; M. Beddall.
Page 37: Imagesource/Creatas; P. Usbeck,
G. P. Bowater/Alamy; Hemera.

Illustrations (page 37): Steve Lillie

No part of this publication may be reproduced in whole or
in part, or stored in a retrieval system, or transmitted in any
form or by any means, electronic, mechanical, photocopying,
recording or otherwise, without written permission of the
publisher. For information regarding permission write to:

Scholastic UK / Mary Glasgow Magazines
Euston House
24 Eversholt Street
London NW1 1DB

© Scholastic Ltd. 2005
This edition reprinted in 2007
All rights reserved.

™&© 2005 Twentieth Century Fox Film Corporation.
All rights reserved.

Printed in Singapore

CONTENTS

	PAGE
Halloween	**4–31**
People and places	4
Chapter 1: A bad day at work	6
Chapter 2: A long, red dress	11
Chapter 3: The fun starts	16
Chapter 4: Who's Buffy?	21
Chapter 5: 'I'm home'	26
Fact Files	**32–37**
Buffy on TV	32
Sarah Michelle Gellar	34
What is Halloween?	36
Self-Study Activities	**38–40**

PEOPLE AND PLACES

HALLOWEEN

THE WATCHER
Rupert Giles
Likes: books, old things

Cordelia Chase
Likes: clothes,
parties, Cordelia!

Angel
How old? 241
Likes: Buffy,
working
against evil

THE SLAYER
Buffy Summers
How old? 16
Likes: Angel, nights
without vampires

THE SLAYERETTES
Willow Rosenberg
Likes: Xander, reading,
helping people

Xander Harris
Likes: Buffy, girls,
having fun

Spike and Drusilla
Like: taking lives, drinking blood

Ethan
Likes: evil plans

PLACES

Sunnydale: A small town in California. Vampires and monsters live there because a door to Hell is under the town. They call it the Hellmouth.
The Bronze: The only cool club in Sunnydale. Teenagers go there in the evenings. They dance, talk and drink coffee.
Sunnydale High: A school for boys and girls from 14 to 18 years. Principal Snyder runs the school.
Ethan's Costume Shop and Party Town: Two shops in Sunnydale with clothes for Halloween and for parties.

HALLOWEEN

CHAPTER 1
A bad day at work

Angel looked at his watch. It was after nine o'clock. 'Where are you, Buffy?' he thought.

The Bronze was busy tonight but Angel sat alone. He looked at the young faces around him. People laughed and danced. 'This is Buffy's world,' he thought. 'Why am I here?' But he already knew the answer. He was there because he loved Buffy.

With his dark eyes, he watched the door.

* * *

Buffy was almost at the Bronze. It was the end of October, two nights before Halloween. The evening was black and cold. Suddenly, something hit Buffy on the back of her head. She turned quickly. A vampire smiled at her –

not a pretty smile. Buffy hit him hard. He got up quickly and laughed. He hit back.

'I haven't got time for this,' Buffy thought. 'Angel is waiting for me.'

She pulled a stake from her jacket. Soon it was in the vampire's body. No more vampire.

'Look at me!' she thought. 'Tonight is my first date with Angel. My clothes are dirty. My hair is terrible. This isn't a good start.'

* * *

'She isn't coming,' thought Angel. He wasn't happy.

'It's like, I *know*,' someone said to him. 'The Bronze just isn't cool. Why do we come here?'

Angel looked up.

'Oh hi, Cordelia,' he said and looked back at the door. 'I'm waiting for Buffy.'

'Great!' she said, and sat down. She smiled and talked. She moved closer to Angel. Angel didn't want her there.

But he was a nice vampire, so he smiled back at her.

It was the wrong time for a smile. Buffy came in and saw them together.

'This is stupid,' she thought. 'Look at Cordelia. She always looks fantastic. And I look … terrible.' She turned to the door.

Angel saw Buffy across the room.

'Buffy?' He ran to the club door.

'Oh … hi,' Buffy said. 'I'm …'

'… late,' Angel finished.

'Bad day at work,' Buffy said.

'Hmm. I see,' said Angel. He smiled.

'I love your hair, Buffy!' Suddenly Cordelia was there. 'Very "street fashion". How do you do it?' She smiled at Buffy then walked back to the table.

'Angel,' said Buffy, 'I'm going to … put a bag over my head. I can't stay here.'

'Don't listen to Cordelia. You look great.'

'You're very kind,' she said. But she didn't believe him.

'We have a date, you know,' laughed Angel.

'A date!' She talked quietly and sadly. 'Other girls have dates. Not me. I never think about my hair and my shoes. I don't have time. I think about vampires and stakes and blood.' She left the club.

Angel didn't follow her. Cordelia came back and smiled.

'Coffee?' she asked.

* * *

The next morning, Principal Snyder waited for the students at Sunnydale High. He had paper and pens.

A girl walked into school. He grabbed her arm.

'Hey!' she said.

'Put your name here,' he told her.

'What is it?' she asked.

'Tomorrow is Halloween, and the children of Sunnydale are going trick-or-treating. They need some teenagers with them. That's you. Put your name here.'

'Can I say "no"?'

'No.'

The girl wrote her name angrily and went off.

'Did you see that?' Xander asked Buffy and Willow.

'Yeah. Let's walk faster,' said Buffy.

'Ah! Miss Summers.' There was a hand on her arm. 'Sunnydale's worst student.' He smiled. 'Put your name here.'

'Oh, I love children, Principal Snyder, but … I'm sorry … there's something wrong with my … ermm … hands. My doctor says …'

Principal Snyder gave her a pen. Then he gave two more pens to Willow and Xander.

'Write! The trick-or-treaters leave here at four o'clock. They must be home at six. Don't forget your costumes.'

* * *

'I don't believe it!' said Xander. 'It's Halloween – party night. And we're going to have lots of small children with us. *And* we're going to be in stupid costumes!'

'I wanted a night at home!' said Buffy. 'It's the only quiet night in the year for me.'

'Halloween is *quiet*?!' Xander was surprised. 'Isn't it party night for vampires?'

'No, they stay at home. Giles told me. '

'I love those vampires,' said Xander.

'So usually I can stay in, too. But now I can't. Thanks, Snyder.'

CHAPTER 2
A long, red dress

At morning break, Buffy and Willow got drinks.

'How was your date last night?' asked Willow.

'Bad,' said Buffy. 'I met a vampire on the way to the Bronze, so I was late. And I looked terrible.'

'Was Angel angry?'

'No, but only because of Cordelia. *She* does dates, not me.'

'Cordelia? Angel doesn't like Cordelia.'

'Willow, what *does* he like? Who is he? I met him a year ago, but I know almost nothing about him.'

'Yeah, well, I don't have any answers,' said Willow.

Then Buffy had an idea. She grabbed Willow. 'The Watcher Diaries*!'

'Yeah …' said Willow slowly. 'And they're Giles's books … in Giles's desk … and Giles is a teacher.'

'You're right,' said Buffy with a smile. 'We mustn't take things from Giles's desk. It's wrong.'

* * *

Buffy and Willow looked through the doors of the library. Giles wasn't there. Willow stayed at the door and Buffy went in.

Buffy walked very quietly to Giles's desk.

'Buffy!' said Giles. 'Good.'

'Oh!' She turned in surprise. 'Nothing! Hi.'

'What?' Giles looked at her. Was she a bit strange today? 'Now, about tomorrow night. Halloween is always quiet. Maybe we can try some new kicks …'

---

* Giles is the Watcher. He writes diaries about Buffy, vampires, monsters and the Hellmouth.

'Giles,' Buffy stopped him. 'Don't you just have fun sometimes?'

'I have lots of fun hobbies,' said Giles, and opened a book. Buffy looked at the door, at Willow. Her eyes said, 'Come in. Get the Watcher Diaries. Giles isn't looking.' Willow's mouth said, 'No!' Buffy's eyes said, 'Now!' Willow walked across the room behind Giles.

'What hobbies?' asked Buffy.

'Well,' Giles started, 'I, -er … sometimes I clean my books. I enjoy that.'

'One day, leave your books for an hour or two, Giles. There's a world out there. There's this cool place. You go in and sit down in the dark. There are pictures on the wall. They move. They tell a story …'

'Very funny, ha ha,' said Giles.

Willow and the Watcher Diaries were back at the door.

'OK, Giles, I gotta go. Bye.' She ran from the room.

* * *

Buffy and Willow sat in the girls' room. They read the Watcher Diaries.

'Wow!' said Buffy. 'Look at her.'

There was a picture of a beautiful woman in a long dress.

'Who is she?' asked Willow.

'It doesn't say. But look! It says 1775 here. Angel was 18 then.'

'She looks very rich,' said Willow.

Buffy thought about Angel in 1775. He was young then, and a man, not a vampire. 'She knew him in the best part of his life. Lucky woman!' she said.

'No!' said Willow. 'Life was terrible for women then.'

The girls' room door opened.

'Well, Buffy, you left poor Angel alone last night.' It was Cordelia. 'He's so nice. But what's his story? I never see him around.'

'Not during the day,' said Willow.

Cordelia looked at Willow.

'He's a vampire. Didn't you know?'

'A nice vampire?! I don't believe you. You can't keep me away from Angel with stupid stories like that. Maybe you're the Vampire Slayer, Buffy, but I'm the Man Slayer around here.'

* * *

'It's so busy in here. You can't move!' shouted Buffy to Willow. They were in Ethan's Costume Shop. Most of Sunnydale's children were there too.

'But it's better than Party Town!' Willow shouted back. Ethan's was new. 'I've got a ghost costume.'

'And I'm getting some soldier clothes and a gun,' said Xander.

'Halloween isn't my …' Buffy stopped. 'Hey! Look at that.'

Willow and Xander followed Buffy to the back of the shop. There they saw a long, red dress.

'It's the dress in the Watcher Diaries,' said Buffy. 'From eighteen-seventy-something.'

'1775,' said Willow. She remembered these things.

'I want it,' said Buffy, quietly.

Suddenly there was a man next to them. It was Ethan Rayne and this was his shop.

'Please,' he said to Buffy. He took the dress and put it against her. 'Ah! Beautiful.' The dress changed Buffy from a pretty girl into a very beautiful woman.

'Wow!' thought Buffy.

'Wow!' said Willow and Xander together.

Buffy woke up. 'I'm sorry,' she said. 'It's too expensive.'

'No, no,' said Ethan. 'Forget the money. You must have it. It's so right for you.'

'Great! Thanks,' said Buffy.

Ethan Rayne smiled.

* * *

The old building was empty. No one lived or worked there now. It wasn't a nice part of town, so the vampires liked it.

Spike walked up and down. 'Buffy,' he thought. 'Buffy must die. Drusilla needs more blood, but that Slayer makes it so difficult.'

'Spike,' someone said quietly.

He turned. His angry face was suddenly kind. It was Drusilla.

'Do you love me?' she asked.

'Come here, my beautiful one,' he said. He put his arms around her weak body.

'Buffy's going to die soon, my love,' he said. 'Then you can drink all the blood in Sunnydale. And you can be strong again.'

'Something is going to happen. I can see it. Buffy is going to be weak.'

'What do you mean? Are there pictures in your head?'

Drusilla closed her eyes.

'Come on, my love. Talk to Spike,' he said. 'What's going to happen to the Slayer? When?'

'Tomorrow,' answered Drusilla.

'But tomorrow is Halloween. Nothing happens on Halloween.'

'This Halloween is different. Someone new is in town.'

CHAPTER 3
The fun starts

Ethan's Costume Shop closed for the night. But Ethan stayed in the shop. He was in the back room, in long, black clothes. In front of him there was a statue with the face of a beautiful woman. He put his hands together. Soon there was blood on them – lots of blood.

He said something to the statue in an old, dead language. 'Janus,' he cried, 'I am your son.'

He walked around to the back of the statue. Here it had another face. But this one wasn't beautiful – it was evil.

* * *

School finished early on Halloween. Soon Buffy was in her costume in her bedroom.

'I'm the woman in the Watcher Diaries,' she thought.

'Where are you meeting Angel?' shouted Willow. She was in the bathroom.

'Here. When the trick-or-treaters go home. Mum's out this evening.'

'Does he know about your costume?'

'No, he doesn't. It's going to be a big surprise! Now, come out, Willow.'

'OK. But don't laugh.'

Buffy didn't laugh. Willow looked fantastic in one of Buffy's tops and a very short skirt.

'Wow!' said Buffy. 'Forget Cordelia. Meet Willow, the new Man Slayer.'

'But this isn't me.' Willow wasn't very happy.

'It's Halloween, Willow. You can be a different person at Halloween – a new you. It's just for one night.'

Someone was at the door.

'Xander's here. Are you ready?'

'Yeah. OK,' said Willow.

Buffy ran down and opened the door. Xander pointed his gun at her.

'Buffy! You are so beautiful!'

'But look at Willow!' said Buffy, and they turned. 'She's … oh …'

Willow was in her costume from Ethan's. '… a ghost.'

* * *

'Let's get our little monsters,' said Xander. They were at Sunnydale High. There were young children in costumes everywhere.

Principal Snyder saw them. He came over to Buffy. Five little people with green faces and black teeth followed him.

'Here's your group, Summers,' he said. He didn't smile. 'Just bring them all back here at six o'clock.'

* * *

Children ran from house to house on the streets of Sunnydale. They shouted and laughed. People answered their doors and looked frightened.

Soon it was nearly six and Buffy's group were tired. Some of them didn't like the dark.

'OK,' she said to them, 'one more house, and then we're going back to school.'

The children ran to another house.

'I'm enjoying this,' she thought. 'It's fun.'

* * *

Back at the costume shop, Ethan was ready for *his* Halloween fun.

'Janus,' he said to the statue, 'this night is yours.'

Buffy was suddenly very cold.

In the next road, Mrs Parker came to her front door. Willow's group waited.

'Trick-or-treat!' they shouted.

'Oh!' Mrs Parker put her hands up. 'I'm so frightened!' Then she smiled. 'What lovely children!'

Ethan took the statue in his hands.

Buffy started to feel a cold wind around her.

A strange green light came from the statue. Ethan smiled. 'Now the fun can start.'

Mrs Parker looked at the trick-or-treaters.

'Well, Mr Monster,' she said to the nearest child. 'What can I … AAAARRRGH!'

A green hand grabbed her neck. The child-monster wasn't a child now. It was a monster – strong and evil.

'What are you doing!? Stop that,' cried Willow.

Mrs Parker pulled the monster's hand off her neck. She ran into the house and closed the door quickly.

Willow suddenly didn't feel right. Her eyes closed. 'I'm falling,' she thought. Then her body was on the floor. She was dead.

* * *

Xander wasn't far away. He started to feel strange, too. Then he was OK. But he was different. He wasn't Xander in a soldier costume – he was a soldier. He was tall and strong. His eyes were cold, and he had a gun.

* * *

Willow sat up. 'What happened?' She walked a little. Then she turned. 'Oh, oh!' Her body – in its ghost costume – was still there. She looked at her clothes – short skirt, short top – Willow the Man Slayer … 'Oh no! I'm a ghost. I'm Willow's ghost.'

She looked down the street. There were frightened children and little monsters everywhere. Then she heard a gun.

'Xander!' She ran to him.

He turned, with his gun on her. He looked like Xander, but something was different.

'It's me. Willow.'

'I don't know a Willow.' He grabbed her arm, but his hand went through her body. 'Hey! What are you?'

'Xander, listen to me. We're friends. Something terrible is happening. I was in a ghost costume, and now I *am* a ghost. You were in a soldier costume, and now you *are* a soldier.'

'I don't believe you.'

A little vampire ran from a house. Xander pointed his gun at it.

'No!' cried Willow. 'There's a little child in there. No guns, OK?'

And then she saw Buffy.

'Buffy, are you all right?'

The little vampire came back. It had a big monster with it this time. They moved nearer.

'Buffy, what do we do?' asked Willow. Buffy looked at the monsters with frightened eyes. And then she started to fall.

CHAPTER 4
Who's Buffy?

Willow looked at Buffy's body on the floor. She didn't believe her eyes.

'Buffy? Are you OK?'

'What? Who is Buffy?' said Buffy.

'She's not Buffy,' Willow said to Xander.

'Who's Buffy?' asked Xander.

'Oh, this is fun,' said Willow. And then to Buffy, 'What year is this?'

Buffy thought. '1775, I believe. I don't understand. Who are you?'

'We're friends. Here, take my hand.'

'Your clothes … everything … is strange,' said Buffy. 'How did I come here?'

Willow looked at Xander. 'What's going to happen to us without the Slayer?' she said.

'What's a Slayer?' asked Xander.

Suddenly a monster kicked Buffy from behind. This new Buffy didn't kick back. She just screamed. Xander hit the monster with his gun and it ran off.

'Let's go into a house,' said Xander.

'Monster!' cried Buffy. 'A monster!'

Willow and Xander

turned. They were ready. But there wasn't a monster. There was only a car.

'It's a car,' said Willow.

'What does it want?' said Buffy.

'What's wrong with this woman?' asked Xander.

'She's from 1775. They didn't have cars then,' said Willow. 'Let's go. Buffy's house is near here.'

Buffy and Xander followed Willow. They went into Buffy's kitchen through the back door. Xander closed the door and watched at the window. 'We're OK … for now.'

BANG, BANG, BANG!

'The front door! Quick!' Xander and Willow ran through the house.

'Don't open it!' said Willow. 'There are vampires out there.'

The sound stopped. Willow and Xander stopped too, and waited.

Buffy came into the room and looked at a photo of a young woman.

'This is just like me,' she said.

'It *is* you,' said Willow. 'Buffy, can't you remember anything?'

'No … no. I don't understand. I don't wear these … these … Are they clothes? I don't like this place. I don't like you. Where is my home?'

Just then a green hand came through the window. It grabbed Xander's arm but he hit it with his gun. The thing ran away.

Now there was a different scream. It wasn't Buffy this time. Xander opened the front door and ran out.

'Hey! Stop!' called Willow. Xander came back. He pulled a woman in a cat costume into the house. She was dirty and there was blood on her arms. It was Cordelia.

'What's happening?' she cried.

'Cordelia!' said Willow. 'OK, now listen. Your name is Cordelia. You're not a cat. You're at high school, and we're your friends … , well …'

'That's nice, Willow,' Cordelia said. 'But I'm not stupid.'

'Do you know us? Oh, that's fantastic,' said Willow.

'Er … yeah,' said Cordelia. 'You're a bit strange today. But look at my costume. Party Town isn't going to like this.'

'OK,' said Willow. 'Cordelia, you stay here with Xander and Buffy. I'm going to see Giles.'

* * *

Willow didn't see Spike in the street. He was under a tree in his long, black coat. His vampire face was evil. He looked around him and smiled.

'Well,' he said, 'this is … great!'

* * *

Xander and Buffy watched the streets from the front door. They were OK … for now. Cordelia watched from a bedroom window.

'Oh, good,' said someone behind them. 'You're all right.'

They turned. It was Angel. 'It's evil out there.'

'Who are you?' they asked.

* * *

'OK,' said Angel, 'what's happening here?' He looked at Buffy's dress. He remembered something … someone … from long ago …

'Do you live here?' asked Xander.

'No! You know that. Buffy …?' This was Buffy … but not Buffy. 'What's up with your hair, Buffy? You look … different,' he said.

'They don't know you, Angel.' It was Cordelia. 'And everyone in the street's a monster.' Then she remembered her smile. 'So, Angel, how are you?'

Someone turned off the lights. Buffy screamed and grabbed Cordelia.

'Hey!' said Cordelia. 'Keep your hands off me!'

Xander turned to Angel.

'Take the girl to the kitchen. Watch the door. Catwoman, stay here with me.'

In the kitchen, the back door was open. 'I closed that,' said Angel. He moved quietly to the door. Buffy stayed by the wall. She didn't see the vampire.

'Be careful!' cried Angel.

He grabbed the vampire and kicked it into the dining room.

'Get a stake!' Angel shouted to Buffy. He turned to her. She saw Angel's face and screamed. It was his vampire face – angry and terrible. She ran out of the house.

'Buffy, no!' shouted Angel. The other vampire hit Angel hard.

* * *

There were a lot of books in front of Giles and Willow.

'This isn't helping,' Willow said. 'What are we looking for?'

'OK,' said Giles. 'Let's think. At six o'clock, everyone changed.'

'Right. So now Xander's a soldier, and Buffy's a girl from 1775.'

Giles looked at Willow. 'And you are …?'

'I'm a ghost,' said Willow.

Giles smiled and looked at her short skirt and top. 'A ghost of …?'

Willow went red. 'You didn't see Cordelia! She has cat ears and …'

'So Cordelia is now a cat?!'

Willow looked at Giles. 'Wait a minute,' she said slowly. 'Cordelia *isn't* a cat. She's the same old Cordelia … in a cat costume.'

'She didn't change, then.'

'No.' Willow thought for a minute. 'I know! Party Town! That's it. Her costume came from Party Town.'

'And you, Buffy, Xander. Where …?'

'We went to this new place,' Willow said. 'Ethan's.'

'Come on!' said Giles. 'Quick!'

CHAPTER 5
'I'm home'

'Hello?' Giles called. 'Is anyone in?'

The shop was dark. Willow saw an open door at the back. There was a statue in the room. It had an evil face with green eyes.

'What does it mean?' she asked.

'It's Janus,' said Giles. 'From an old world. Janus has two faces – man and woman, good and evil …'

'Milk and dark …' Ethan was just behind them. Willow and Giles turned quickly. 'Oh no, sorry. That's chocolate.'

Ethan smiled at Giles.

'Willow,' Giles said. He didn't look at her. 'Go to Buffy. Now.'

'But …'

'Now, Willow.'

She turned and ran.

'Hello, Ethan.'

'Hello, Rupert, my old friend,' Ethan answered. 'This

is nice.'

Giles didn't smile. 'I was stupid. I didn't think of you. But of course this Halloween thing is your idea. It's just like all your other plans.'

'Yes,' Ethan said. 'All my plans are clever.'

'Not clever, Ethan – evil.'

'Well, Rupert, you know all about evil, of course.' He laughed. 'But maybe they don't know about you here.'

Giles changed. No one in Sunnydale knew this Giles.

'Stop your evil, Ethan. Then leave this place. Never come here again.'

'Oooooh. I'm frightened …'

Giles hit him. Ethan went down hard onto the floor. There was blood on his mouth.

* * *

Angel's vampire face changed, and he looked like a man again. He found Xander and Cordelia and they ran into the road.

'Buffy, Buffy, where are you?' Angel called.

'Let's go this way,' said Xander.

'She needs help – now,' Angel said. 'I know it.'

'Buffy's always OK,' said Cordelia.

'But this isn't Buffy …'

* * *

Spike watched them. He had two small vampires with him.

'Did you hear that, my friends? Drusilla was right. Tonight Buffy is weak. Come on. We must find her first. Then we can drink that lovely blood.'

* * *

Buffy was alone on a dark street in the bad part of town. She was very frightened.

She ran into something … someone. He was big and dirty, with bad teeth.

'Pretty … pretty,' he said, and grabbed Buffy. 'Mmm,' he said. 'Nice.'

'No!' cried Buffy.

Xander suddenly arrived. 'Hey!' he shouted, and pulled the man off Buffy. Buffy screamed and ran … right into Cordelia.

Then Buffy saw Angel. She screamed again and grabbed Cordelia.

'What's up with you?' Cordelia cried.

'That man! Your friend! He's … he's a *vampire*!' she screamed.

Cordelia smiled at Angel. 'She thinks … oh, forget it.'

Then she turned to Buffy. 'It's OK. Angel is … a friend. He likes us.'

'Hey!' They all turned. It was Willow.

'We gotta get out of the road,' she said.

'This way.' Angel ran to an old building.

The others followed him into the building and closed the door. But Spike was just behind them, with a lot of little vampires. They kicked the door and it opened. Spike came into the building. He smiled at his little helpers.

* * *

Ethan had lots of blood on his face, but he smiled too.

'How do I stop this evil?' Giles asked. He cleaned the blood from his hands.

Ethan laughed. 'Say "please".'

Giles kicked him.

'OK. OK! B-B-Break Janus,' said Ethan. 'B-Break the statue.'

* * *

Vampires pulled Angel and Xander away. Spike turned to Buffy. 'My little one,' he said. 'Frightened. Alone. No one can help you now.'

He smiled kindly. Then he hit her across the face.

'I'm enjoying this,' he laughed.

'Buffy!' Angel cried. But the vampires pulled him harder.

Spike grabbed Buffy's head with one hand. He had her arm in the other. His long white teeth came close to her beautiful neck.

* * *

Giles ran to the back room. He grabbed the statue and hit it against the floor. Bits of statue went everywhere. He looked for Ethan. But he wasn't there.

* * *

Suddenly Spike's vampires weren't vampires. They were high school students and little trick-or-treaters again.

Spike still had Buffy's head in his hand.

'Hi!' she said to Spike. 'I'm home.'

Spike didn't look happy now. Buffy was the Vampire Slayer again, and she was very angry. She kicked him and hit him. Then she kicked him again.

'Do you know something?' she said. 'I'm enjoying this!'

Spike hit the floor hard and didn't move again.

'Hey, Buff!' said Xander. 'We're back!'

'Do you remember anything?' asked Cordelia.

'Yeah,' said Xander. 'It was like, "I'm here. I can hear you. But I can't get out." It was strange.'

'Are you OK?' Angel asked Buffy quietly. Buffy looked into his dark eyes. She loved those eyes.

'Yeah,' she smiled. He took her arm and they went out.

'Hey!' said Xander. 'Where's Willow?'

* * *

'What happened?' asked Willow. She was at Mrs Parker's house in her ghost costume.

'Well, I'm in my own body again,' she thought. 'That feels better.'

* * *

Buffy was in Buffy clothes with Buffy hair again. She was at home, with Angel. She sat down next to him.

'I like this Buffy,' he said. 'I hated the girls in the old days.'

'Did you?'

'They were boring. I want someone … exciting.' He moved closer. 'Interesting.'

'Oh yeah?'

'Strong.'

Then he took her in his arms. And Buffy smiled. 'This feels right,' she thought.

* * *

The next day, Giles was in Ethan's empty shop. He walked around slowly. Suddenly he saw some paper. There were words on it. 'See you soon,' he read. Giles looked up. His eyes were hard and cold.

FACT FILE

BUFFY ON TV

☾ *Buffy* was first on television in 1997. Lots of TV programmes stop after one season. Not *Buffy*. There are seven seasons of *Buffy*. People watch it all around the world. There are fan clubs and books – and there's a *Buffy* doll too. What is special about *Buffy*? A girl slays vampires. Who cares?

Well, *Buffy* isn't just about vampires. It's frightening, but it's also funny. And it's about life. It's about teenagers, their loves, their hopes, their problems. But one thing is different. These teenagers – Buffy, Cordelia, Willow, Xander – live in a very strange world.
Read more at **www.bbc.co.uk/cult/buffy.**

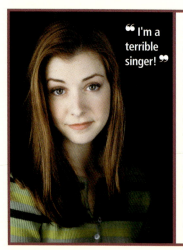

"I'm a terrible singer!"

☀ One *Buffy* programme in Season 6, 'Once More, With Feeling', is a musical. A monster arrives in Sunnydale. His name is Sweet and he likes music. He puts a curse on everyone. Under the curse, they can't talk. They can only sing. But in the end, Buffy breaks the curse and Sweet leaves town. Only one of the people in the programme doesn't sing much: Willow (actor Alyson Hannigan). Alyson thinks she's a terrible singer.

☾ *Halloween* is Programme 6 from Season 2.

☀ They film each *Buffy* programme in only eight days.

Do you watch *Buffy*? Why/Why not?

THE PROGRAMME

David Boreanaz

🌙 One Halloween, friends asked Alyson Hannigan to a Halloween party. The *Buffy* make-up man changed her into a vampire. She looked very real. Her friends didn't know her.

☀ Real bands play at the Bronze. New bands send their CDs to the makers of *Buffy*. The *Buffy* music people listen to the CDs and choose the best ones. Then those bands come and play on the programme.

🌙 David Boreanaz plays Angel. They tested lots of actors for Angel, but didn't like any of them. It was the day before the start of work on the first *Buffy* programme, 'Welcome to the Hellmouth!', and they still didn't have an actor for Angel. Someone saw David through a window and shouted, 'That guy! Can you see him? He's taking his dog for a walk. He's Angel!' And soon he was.

The Bronze

What do these words mean? You can use a dictionary.
real   a programme   a season   a fan club   a doll   a curse   an actor   make-up

FACT FILE

Sarah Michelle Gellar

❝ Why is *Buffy* so great? Because you can understand so many of the characters. You have the same problems, and you feel the same about them. ❞

Sarah Michelle Gellar

Started life: April 1977 in New York City, USA
Friends call her: Sassy
How tall? 1.6 metres (like Buffy)
First job as an actor: 1981
First film: 1983
First *Buffy* programme: 1997
Love life: husband is Freddie Prinze Jr, also an actor – they starred together in the films *Scooby Doo* and *Scooby Doo II*
Pets: two dogs
Hobbies: old books (don't tell Giles!), kickboxing and lots of other sports
Favourite food: sushi
Favourite country: Japan
Family: no brothers or sisters

Q How did you get the job of Buffy?
A The makers of *Buffy* knew about me from other TV work. They wanted actors for all the *Buffy* characters and they tested me for Cordelia.

Q So what happened? Did they like you?
A I think so. But I wanted to play Buffy. So I said, 'Can you test me for Buffy?'

Q What did they say?
A 'Yes.' But I didn't get the job the first time. Lots of other girls wanted to be Buffy too. They tested me 17 times – but I got the job in the end.

> Is Sarah Michelle Gellar a good actor, do you think? Why/Why not?

THE STARS

Buffy & Angel

In 'Halloween', Buffy and Angel have their first date. But Angel is a vampire and Buffy is the Vampire Slayer! How does that work?

"I slay vampires. That's my job."

"I can walk like a man, but I'm not one."

Q Who is Buffy?
A Well, her name is Buffy Summers. She lives with her mother. Her father left them and she has no brothers or sisters. Her first job as Slayer was when she was 15. At that time she was at Hemery High School in Los Angeles. She found vampires in the school but no one believed her. There was a fire. The teachers didn't want Buffy at their school after that. So she came to Sunnydale High School.

Q Who is Angel?
A He's older than Buffy – 241 years old. His family came from Ireland and they had lots of money. But one day he met Darla, a vampire, and she bit him. Now he was a vampire too. Vampires don't care about anything. They don't have a soul. He went all over the world and took the lives of many people. In Romania in 1898, he took the life of a lovely young girl. Her family were very sad and angry. They put a curse on Angel – they gave him a soul. He can never be happy. He feels very sorry about his old, evil life. He wants to help the Slayer. He came to California because of this.

Q Why does Buffy love Angel? He's a vampire!
- Because he's dark and good-looking.
- Because he's alone. She's alone too. She has good friends, but she feels different from them. She is the only Slayer.
- Because he helps her. He hates evil too.

What do these words mean? You can use a dictionary.

a character   kickboxing   to bite (*past* bit)   **a soul**

FACT FILE

What is H

Halloween started more than 2000 years ago, but it had a different name in those days: Samain. At that time the people of Britain were Celts. Samain was the last day of the Celtic year and 1 November was the first day of the new year. The Celts believed in ghosts – and the ghosts all came out on Samain. November was the month of the dead.

In AD 835, the Christian church made Samain a Christian day. They called it 'All Hallows Eve'. The name Halloween comes from this.

What happens at Halloween?

At Halloween in the UK and US, children and teenagers dress in frightening costumes. They go to people's houses and shout 'Trick or treat!' Sometimes the person in the house gives them a 'treat' – usually sweets or money. Then the children go to the next house. Sometimes the person in the house just closes the door. Then the children decide on a 'trick' – they break eggs on the front door or do other bad things.

THE FACTS

alloween?

Who do you agree with?

"I buy lots of sweets for Halloween. It's expensive."

"We're frightened. The teenagers aren't nice to us. They break eggs on our windows."

"I love seeing the children in their costumes. They're always smiling and excited. It's a fun evening for them and it's nice for older people."

"Sweets are bad for children. They eat too many already."

"It's the best night of the year. I love the costumes. I love the dark. And I love the sweets!"

Also at Halloween …

☾ At bedtime, put your shoes in the shape of the letter 'T'. Go to sleep and remember your dream. The boy or girl in your dream is going to be your husband or wife.

☾ Who do you love? Find out on 31 October – Halloween. Take the peel off a fruit in one long piece. Throw it behind you. What letter does it make? The name of your true love starts with this letter.

What do these words mean? You can use a dictionary.
sweets   to throw   an egg   peel   a piece

SELF-STUDY ACTIVITIES

CHAPTERS 1-2

Before you read

You can use your dictionary for these questions.

1 Match these words with the words in *italics* in the sentences.
**costumes   a diary   grab   ghosts
trick-or-treaters   blood   a stake**
   a) You can use *this* to kill a vampire.
   b) *Take* the last cake on the plate *quickly*.
   c) Children often wear vampire *clothes* at Halloween.
   d) Vampires have to drink *this* or they die.
   e) Willow writes about her life in *this*.
   f) Lots of *these* come to our door at Halloween.
   g) Some people believe in *these*. Some people don't believe in them. Do you?

2 Choose the right answer.
   a) Which of these people often uses a gun in their work?
      i a teacher   **ii** a soldier   **iii** a doctor   **iv** a student
   b) Which of these do you find in a library?
      i beds   **ii** guitars   **iii** trains   **iv** vegetables   **v** books
   c) You go with your girlfriend/boyfriend to the cinema.
      What do we call this?
      i a time   **ii** a date   **iii** a team   **iv** a week   **v** a month
   d) What do you use when you kick something?
      i your hand   **ii** your head   **iii** your mouth   **iv** your foot

3 What does 'weak' mean?
   Which of these people is going to be weak in the story?
   i Buffy   **ii** Angel   **iii** Willow   **iv** Xander   **v** Giles   **vi** Cordelia

After you read

4 Choose the correct words.
   a) Angel has a date with *Cordelia / Buffy*.
   b) Buffy leaves Angel at the Bronze because she *doesn't like him / looks terrible*.
   c) Xander and Buffy *are / are not* happy about Principal

Snyder's plans for Halloween.
- **d)** Giles *sees / doesn't see* Willow in the library.
- **e)** Spike is Drusilla's *boyfriend / father*.

5 What do you think?
- **a)** Is Angel going to go on a date with Cordelia?
- **b)** Buffy is going to wear the dress from 1775. What's going to happen to her then?
- **c)** Drusilla says, 'Someone new is in town.' Who is it?

CHAPTERS 3-4

Before you read

You can use your dictionary for these questions.

6 Think of a statue in your town or city. Who/What is it and where is it? Are there any statues in your school?

7 Complete the sentences with these words.

evil   monster   neck   strange   scream
- **a)** Thud is big and green. He's got six eyes and two heads. He's a … .
- **b)** People … when they meet Thud on a dark night.
- **c)** Thud is very, very, very bad – he is … .
- **d)** Your … is between your head and your body; Thud has two of these.
- **e)** Thud can't eat chocolate. When he eats it, he feels very … .

After you read

8 Correct these sentences.
- **a)** Willow goes out in a Man Slayer costume.
- **b)** When Ethan calls Janus, the trick-or-treaters change into children.
- **c)** Xander doesn't know Willow, and Willow doesn't know Xander.
- **d)** Cordelia is a cat.
- **e)** Buffy screams because Angel kicks the vampire.
- **f)** Cordelia's costume didn't come from Party Town.

SELF-STUDY ACTIVITIES

9 What do you think?
- **a)** Who is Ethan Rayne and why is he in town?
- **b)** Willow changes into a ghost. Buffy changes into a woman from 1775. Xander changes into a soldier. How are they going to change back into Willow, Buffy and Xander?
- **c)** Which is better: your own life in the 21st century, or the life of rich people in 1775? Why?

CHAPTER 5

Before you read

10 What are they doing right now? Match the two columns.

a) Giles and Willow are	**i**	running from Angel.
b) Buffy is	**ii**	trying to hit a vampire.
c) Xander and Cordelia are	**iii**	going to Ethan's.
d) Angel is	**iv**	watching for vampires.

11 Will Angel ask Buffy on another date in this story?

After you read

12 Complete the sentences with these names.

Buffy Giles Angel Janus Willow Ethan Cordelia

- **a)** … knew Giles before he came to Sunnydale.
- **b)** … hits Ethan very hard.
- **c)** … doesn't know that Angel is a vampire.
- **d)** Spike wants to drink …'s blood.
- **e)** Giles breaks the statue of … .
- **f)** … is suddenly at Mrs Parker's house.
- **g)** … doesn't want the girl from 1775 – he wants Buffy.

13 What do you think?
- **a)** Is Angel a good boyfriend for Buffy? Why/Why not?
- **b)** Willow, Xander and Cordelia know about the vampires in Sunnydale. Why don't they move to a different town?
- **c)** What does Ethan know about Giles from his life before Sunnydale?